25 Essential Bible Verses for Christian Business Leaders

Reflective Journal Volume I

1 Chronicles 12:32: "...*of the sons of Issachar who had understanding of the times, to know what Israel ought to do.*"

1 John 2:20: "*But ye have an unction from the Holy One, and ye know all things.*"

Vision for the Reflective Journal

I am writing this book to help Christian leaders in the workplace. I want to share how I applied foundational management principles that I found in the Bible to bring me success in the workplace.

This journal is intended to be a tool to serve you as a Christian leader to help you grow in wisdom and grow in your ability to use the Scriptures and the leading of the Holy Spirit to guide you to success in whatever leadership position in which you find yourself.

I have called it a journal because I hope that

certain entries will cause you to pause and reflect on your leadership style and approach to certain things and take a few notes that will help you become more successful.

The cool thing I have found about journal entries is that you can stir yourself up all over again by going back and rereading something that you previously received while reflecting, something that impressed you or struck you a certain way. When you reread an entry, you can also see what you thought about something at a certain point in your growth as a leader and see if you are progressing.

Your journal entries will then challenge you, encourage you, and push you to be a better leader. Your journal entries can also serve as the basis for brief teaching sessions as you help train the leaders who are under you to become better leaders.

Every leader should be growing. Luke 2:52 says, "Jesus increased in wisdom and stature and in favor with God and man." Every leader should be growing in wisdom, increasing in their ability to lead, learning how to apply the things they've learned to make great decisions faster and increasing their internal capacity to deal with typical leadership pressures.

To my young leaders, I sincerely desire that this

journal will make you better prepared to face the challenges that all leaders will eventually face.

Introduction

As a young leader, I figured that if there was an important leadership lesson or an essential managerial principle I needed to learn, I could learn it from God through the leading of the Holy Spirit and find it in the Bible. Why?

I knew that God was the greatest manager that ever lived. I knew that He kept the universe in perfect alignment daily and simultaneously held all of our souls in life while also knowing our most intimate thoughts, the number of hairs on our heads, and even the exact number of all our days. This revelation was an important starting point for me because, as a new leader/supervisor, I felt a lot of pressure to learn this "new" management theory or that new management philosophy. I was starting to feel like I was behind because I hadn't read the "latest" books.

Then I believe the Holy Spirit led me to Ecclesiastes 1:9-10 which say, "And there is nothing new under the sun. Is there anything of which it may be said, See, this is new? It has already been in ancient times before us." This Scripture confirmed for me that there isn't anything new.

Everything that the "authors" of new management theories were presenting had its underpinnings in something that existed before. These new management theories were merely previously existing biblical principles repackaged with new terms.

Armed with this premise, I knew there had to be a set of enduring management and leadership principles hidden somewhere in the Bible. I knew that if I studied the great leaders of the Bible, people such as Joshua, Moses, Daniel, Joseph, Esther, etc., these principles had to be in there.

Intuitively, I also knew that Jesus had a leadership style I could learn from. I knew God had to be guiding the great leaders of old by His wisdom and the very principles by which He was successfully directing the affairs of the universe.

I'm not saying don't read books, leadership, and management journals and articles. Exactly the opposite, I encourage it. Sometimes, an author may take one of these enduring principles and put a new twist on it that helps you understand how to apply it better.

When I was reading, if I found an author's "new" management nugget or leadership model to be really good, I would force myself to go back and find its roots in Scripture. Again, my underlying premise was that if it was good or sound, it had to be in the Scriptures--it had to have existed before because "there is nothing new under the sun."

By forcing myself to find the biblical origins of key managerial/leadership principles, I gained a better understanding of these principles. Moreover, as I was reading the Scriptures, the Holy Spirit was teaching me.

> **John 14:26**: *"But the Comforter, which is the Holy Ghost, whom the Father will send in my name, he shall teach you all things, and bring all things to your remembrance, whatsoever I have said unto you."*

> **John 16:13**: *"Howbeit when he, the Spirit of truth, is come, he will guide you into all truth: for he shall not speak of himself; but whatsoever he shall hear, that shall he speak: and he will shew you things to come."*

As I read the scriptural foundation for a principle such as delegation, the Holy Spirit would elaborate on it so that I could understand it better. Further, the Holy

Spirit would help me understand how a modern-day author applied it in their "new" model and, most importantly, guide me in applying that principle in my current leadership position. It was amazing to me. I was beginning to grasp management and leadership principles that people had read mountains of books to grasp.

It should make sense that if I have the wisdom of God from the Scriptures and the leading of the Holy Spirit, I should have amazing results in the workplace-- and I did. I will share some of those in this volume of the book, and in the volumes that will follow. My first real example of this came when I began to study what the Bible said about vision.

In 1991, I was working in a job on a general officer's Total Quality Management (TQM) staff. TQM was the latest management "fad" if you will, and I was working in the job when TQM was in its heyday in the Air Force. I remember when Dr. Joseph M. Duran, a world-renowned authority on "quality," was brought to our base to consult our senior generals on management. The use of Dr. Deming's management principles was also at an all-time high.

My office mates all attended very expensive Deming and Juran training to grasp these new principles. They told me it was too expensive to send me and that

I'd have to learn from my coworkers or attend a lesser class. I remember going to a class put on by the General Services Administration (GSA) and thinking that not only was I far behind in my learning but that I wasn't going to get the opportunity to go to the best classes to catch up.

I was trying to read all of Deming and Juran's books and feverishly reading magazine and journal articles. It seemed insurmountable. At about that same time, I got the revelation that "there was nothing new under the sun." I began spending more of my time in Scripture trying to find the biblical underpinnings for the "new" TQM management philosophy.

I believe the Holy Spirit led me specifically to study vision. I'd seen many articles and books about vision and mission and many terms that overlapped these same words. That's when I first applied the process of finding the biblical underpinnings for a managerial/leadership tenet. Here are the steps in my process.

I start by letting the Holy Spirit expound on the principle until it becomes a revelation with deep understanding in my heart. I allow the Holy Spirit to show me how other modern-day authors used the principle. Finally, I let the Holy Spirit guide me in applying the principle in my workplace.

When I followed these steps, I got such an astonishing revelation of the concept of vision that I began to write it all down. Writing it down, however, wasn't enough, so I felt compelled to share it.

I wrote a paper on the use of vision and TQM in the workplace. I was then led to submit it to the American Society for Quality Control's (ASQC) Annual Quality Congress. My paper, "Vision the Missing Factor in the Quality Equation," was not only accepted by the ASQC for inclusion in its published papers, but I was invited to attend the 43rd Annual National Quality Congress as a guest speaker.

As a speaker, I elaborated on the topic of vision primarily from the revelations I had gotten from Scripture. Then, I worked backward to put some of the material in my presentation into the "new" TQM language of the time. I also carefully sprinkled in the Scriptural tenets without saying "the Bible says" because it was a secular event. People came up to me afterward, excited about my presentation. I remember almost laughing to myself saying I'm speaking at this national conference on the wisdom and revelation that I got from the Bible.

When I returned, my two-star general called me into his office to discuss my paper. It created quite a ruckus because he told me to come alone. To put this in perspective, I worked for a major who worked for a civilian GM-15, the equivalent of a full Colonel, and he worked for a senior executive service member who was equivalent to a one-star general. None of them were allowed to attend.

The two-star wanted to discuss my thoughts on organizational vision during a time when "quality" was in its heyday, and we had a whole quality staff headed up by a general officer equivalent. I honestly felt like Daniel or Joseph, but I knew I couldn't take credit for the insights I had written in the paper.

I'd gotten those insights primarily from listening to the Holy Spirit expound on just a few Scriptures. The Holy Spirit also gave me graphical depictions to share in my presentation that added greater depth to what I had learned.

As you go through this journal, I encourage you to follow the same process I did. Use what I have written as a start, and then let the Holy Spirit expound on the Scripture for you and tailor-make implementations of the principles specific to your leadership situation. Write down what you believe you hear the Holy Spirit speaking to you about what revelation you have received and what specific actions you are supposed to take.

Hearing the voice of the Holy Spirit is a God-given

spiritual ability that you work at and refine over time. I highly recommend the book "A Guide for Listening and Inner-Healing Prayer" by Rusty Rustenbach as a resource for refining your inner ear, the ability to hear the Holy Spirit speak to you in your heart. I can guarantee that you will never get better at listening to the voice of the Holy Spirit by not trying.

The best way to approach listening prayer is to quiet your heart from the busyness and clamor that make up your daily responsibilities. Maybe take some weekend morning or part of a lunch break and sit in the presence of God, meditate on a Scripture provided in this journal or some other Scriptures, and then listen inside your heart for what the Holy Spirit will say. Jesus described this process in the following Scripture:

> **Luke 10:38-42**: "Now it came to pass, as they went, that he entered into a certain village: and a certain woman named Martha received him into her house. And she had a sister called Mary, which also sat at Jesus' feet, and heard his word. But Martha was cumbered about much serving, and came to him, and said, Lord, dost thou not care that my sister hath left me to serve alone? bid her therefore that she help me. And Jesus answered and said unto her, Martha, Martha,

thou art careful and troubled about many things: But one thing is needful: and Mary hath chosen that good part, which shall not be taken away from her."

There is a time for multi-tasking, and there is a time to sit in awe and reverence for the awesome presence of God. To be blown away all over again that the God of the universe would make time to talk to you about matters of great consequence to you but don't even register on the scale of eternal importance.

It is the love of a good Father to pay attention to what's important to His child; that's real love on display, and we can all come to know and benefit from it. Leanne Payne has a fantastic book on this subject, "Listening Prayer: Learning to Hear God's Voice and Keep a Prayer Journal." Another good book that describes this type of "listening prayer" is "The Practice of the Presence of God" by Brother Lawrence. It is a powerful yet incredibly inexpensive book.

If none of what I said about hearing the voice of God in your daily life registers with you, I pray that you search for an understanding of the Scriptures and pray to God directly until it does. Having fellowship and two-way dialogue with the living God is your Christian privilege. Other than eternal salvation and the gift of the Holy Spirit, it is probably the greatest benefit of becoming a Christian. Please share your success stories with me at ivan.arizona@yahoo.com.

I will close this chapter with this Scripture from Daniel 11:32 "...but the people that do know their God shall be strong, and do exploits." Now go out with God's scriptural wisdom and the Holy Spirit's leading and do exploits!

25 Essential Bible Verses for Christian Business Leaders Reflective Journal Volume 1

Chapter 1 Delegation

Exodus 18:14 – 26: *"So when Moses' father-in-law saw all that he did for the people, he said, 'What is this thing that you are doing for the people? Why do you alone sit, and all the people stand before you from morning until evening?' And Moses said to his father-in-law, 'Because the people come to me to inquire of God. When they have a difficulty, they come to me, and I judge between one and another; and I make known the statutes of God and His laws.' So Moses' father-in-law said to him, 'The thing that you do is not good. Both you and these people who are with you will surely wear yourselves out. For this thing is too much for you; you are not able to perform it by yourself. Listen now to my voice; I will give you counsel, and God will be with you: Stand before God for the people, so that you may bring the difficulties to God. And you shall teach them the statutes and the laws, and show them the way in which they must walk* *and the work they must do. Moreover you shall select from all the people able men, such as fear God, men of truth, hating covetousness; and place such over them to be rulers of thousands, rulers of hundreds, rulers of fifties, and rulers of tens. And let them judge the people at all times. Then it will be that every great matter they shall bring to you, but every small matter they themselves shall judge. So it will be easier for you, for they will bear the burden with you. If you do this thing, and God so commands you, then you will be able to endure, and all this people will also go to their place in peace.' So Moses heeded the voice of his father-in-law and did all that he had said. And Moses chose able men out of all Israel, and made them heads over the people: rulers of thousands, rulers of hundreds, rulers of fifties, and rulers of tens. So they judged the people at all times; the hard cases they brought to Moses, but they judged every small case themselves."*

There are so many good lessons in delegation, grooming, mentoring, and other leadership areas in this passage. I want to make sure that you get them all. The first lesson is a lesson in humility, and it is the key that unlocks everything else. Moses is the leader of the children of Israel. God speaks to him face to face. Yet he humbled himself to be able to take some good advice from his father-in-law.

It would have been very easy for Moses to resist his father-in-law's advice based on the fact he heard from God face to face; he had just led 2 million people out of Egyptian bondage and worked some of the greatest miracles that had ever been seen.

We all have blind spots, areas where we can't see. Are you willing to take advice or critiques from someone "lower" than you? Lower could be a position in the company in terms of job title or experience. It could be someone with a lower level of education.

It also could be possible that you look differently on advice from people that have a different gender, race, political or other preferences. That is something you need to consider that carefully and make a painstakingly honest assessment.

If there are serious issues in this area, you may have to share them with a trusted friend to help you be accountable as you make progress. Why? Because you never know who can see the things in your blind spot. As a leader, you can't afford arrogance. It will cause you to miss important insights, most notably the things that are in your blind spot.

Delegation thought. How do you know when you're not delegating enough? How do you know when what is on your management plate is too much? A sure sign is when you are working overtime all the time.

When everything "big and small" has to come to you for review and approval.

Delegation and grooming thought. If you have no one you can delegate to, and no direct reports that you can trust to handle simple matters without consulting you, then you have one of the following problems. You have either failed to hire the right people, failed to develop the people you hired, or failed to communicate the vision and goals in such a way that they could "run" with little direct supervision and complete tasks within the spirit of the organization's vision and stated goals. (see Habakkuk 2:2: "And the LORD answered me, and said, Write the vision, and make it plain upon tables, that he may run that readeth it.")

Grooming, mentoring, and professional development thoughts. Jethro told Moses to choose "able men." A closer look shows that he told them to choose men of character and ability.

What processes do you have in place to identify men and women of character and ability? What systems exist within your organization to assess the various capacities of each of your folks? Do these systems feed that type of info back to you, or is it buried, or perhaps even scattered in various places and therefore rendered unusable?

What databases, processes, and meetings would you have to bring together to regularly feed this information back to you in some useful fashion?

When you have that kind of information fed back to you, you can more effectively answer the question that Jethro asked Moses: Who are the people of character and ability that you can set over 10s, 50s, and 100s?

More systems thoughts. What systems do you have in place to prove or test leadership/management capacity? How are you developing leaders to grow to their max capacity, be it 10s, 50s, or 100s? How do you know when you have set someone in place beyond their capability? How do you fix it since it was your decision to do so?

Longevity. Regarding failing to delegate, Jethro told Moses, "The thing that you do is not good. Both you and these people who are with you will surely wear yourselves out." He later said about effective delegation: "If you do this thing, and God so commands you, then you will be able to endure." It's a matter of longevity. Longevity has many facets. I saw a senior leader develop heart issues due to working 17-18 hours a day because he could not effectively delegate.

He had arrogance, which may have been unknown to him, and manifested itself in the thinking that the best decisions only came from him. Armed with that thinking, he had to see everything. Jethro would say he could not keep "the great matters" for himself to decide while delegating the "small" matters.

I'm thinking of the longevity of marriages and families cut short because someone could not delegate effectively and allowed time to be stolen from their family. Many of you have heard the expression, "no one on their deathbed wishes they had spent more time at work."

I worked for a general who could not distinguish between "great" and "small" matters. He was wearing his staff out as they gathered details on small matters and constantly fed them to him to satisfy his nearly insatiable appetite for details.

It took a few years, but ultimately, his appetite for details on small things obscured his ability to see the details on great things. Some units under his purview failed several critical inspections and gained national attention. He received a curtailment in his longevity in the form of a demotion in rank. It was easily avoidable through effective delegation.

Failure to delegate does have a very tangible cost. It has a cost regarding your health, the health of your most prized relationships, and even your career's longevity.

Reflection/Call to Action: What things can you delegate today? How do you need to improve the way that you delegate? What are the mid and long-term things (processes, personnel) that might need to change for you to delegate more effectively? Out of all these reasons for delegating more effectively, which ones most apply to you?

_____

_____

_____

_____

_____

_____

_____

_____

_____

25 Essential Bible Verses for Christian Business Leaders

Reflective Journal Volume 1

Chapter 2 Leadership

Isaiah 9:16: *"For the leaders of this people cause them to err..."*

Luke 14:28: *"For which of you, intending to build a tower, does not sit down first and count the cost, whether he has enough to finish it?"*

Dr. W. Edwards Deming is a famous management guru who went to Japan after World War II and taught management principles to leaders of prominent Japanese businesses. After implementing these principles, "businesses like Toyota, Fuji, and Sony saw great success... and by the 1970s, many of these companies dominated the global market." (Mind Tools Editorial Team, n.d.)

One of Dr. Deming's most famous points of emphasis is that it all starts with leadership. He would say that we are quick to blame workers or some other area, but he felt that leadership should shoulder most of the blame.

If you think about it, leadership is responsible for hiring decisions and the organization's vision, goals, and strategies used to reach the goals. Leaders decide which policies are implemented, how the money is spent, where the people are placed within the organization, etc. Like Dr. Deming, the Scripture says that the people "do err" because of their leaders. So why do we look everywhere but at the leaders when something is going wrong?

As leaders, we must ask ourselves, have I communicated the vision clearly enough? Have I clearly communicated our strategy to accomplish our goals?" Have I allocated enough resources (people, equipment, $) to accomplish our goals? Have I made myself available to provide timely inputs, permission, and clarification? Am I a good listener? Are people afraid to talk to me? Do they perceive me as trustworthy and fair?

We must also ask ourselves if the managers we have put in place share my values, goals, and desire to empower the people at the lower levels to get things done. Am I growing as the company grows in my ability to delegate and share the glory of success and the responsibility for failure? Am I growing in my ability to develop those under me to handle greater responsibilities?

Reflection: What things jumped out and grabbed you? What things might you need to be accountable for with a trusted peer?

_____
_____
_____
_____
_____
_____
_____
_____
_____
_____
_____

Proverbs 29:2: *"When the righteous are in authority, the people rejoice: but when the wicked beareth rule, the people mourn."*

Romans 13:3-4: *"For rulers are not a terror to good works, but to evil. Do you want to be unafraid of the authority? Do what is good, and you will have praise from the same. For he is God's minister to you for good. But if you do evil, be afraid; for he does not bear the sword in vain; for he is God's minister, an avenger to execute wrath on him who practices evil."*

The idea here is that Christian leadership in the workplace should make a difference. There should be things that the people in the workplace should not have to experience: racism, sexism, favoritism, or workplace violence. Any occurrence of these things should be dealt with swiftly and courageously. Courage may be needed to take actions that demonstrate unequivocally that these types of things will not be tolerated.

There are some things that should be present because you are there: a sense of direction and purpose, a sense of fairness, encouragement, enthusiasm, relative peace, freedom to be creative, and permission for everyone in the workplace to do their very best. There should also be an assurance that good work will be rewarded to all regardless of gender, race, age, physical or other disabilities.

Reflection: Do you see yourself as a courageous leader? Would the people that you lead describe you as courageous? What things or people have you put off confronting? Are you "too comfortable" confronting? Specifically, does your confrontation style also convey a sense of concern for the individual and the organization? If you have a quick confrontation "trigger," have there been a lot of casualties and collateral damage? How could you strike a better balance between needed confrontation and conveying in a genuine way that the person has value both to you and the organization?

_____

_____

_____

_____

_____

_____

_____

_____

1 Timothy 5:19: *"Against an elder receive not an accusation, but before two or three witnesses."*

1 Peter 2:17-18: *"Show proper respect to everyone, love the family of believers, fear God, honor the emperor. Slaves, in reverent fear of God submit yourselves to your masters, not only to those who are good and considerate, but also to those who are harsh."*

Romans 13:7: *"Render therefore to all their dues: tribute to whom tribute is due; custom to whom custom; fear to whom fear; honour to whom honour."*

One of the hardest things to do as a boss is not to bad mouth or criticize your higher-level bosses in front of your subordinates. Let me explain. It is very common for a lower-level supervisor to say something like, "yeah higher-level management doesn't know what they are doing. They make all these policies but don't have a clue what we do down here." It is also very common for supervisors to pass the blame on higher-level bosses: "I tried to get that policy changed and get us newer equipment and get us more overtime hours, but the higher-level bosses said no."

It might very well be true that the higher-level bosses said no, but as a lower-level supervisor, it is critical how you relay the information. A look at the Scriptures provided says that we should reverence, show respect for, and show honor for those in authority. 1 Timothy 2:1-2 even say we are supposed to pray for those in authority. So, let's look at some examples of applications of these spiritual truths.

One of your folks comes up and says, "Hey I heard that the higher-level bosses disapproved our recommendations!" That kind of falls in line with 1 Timothy 5 and "not receiving an accusation against an elder." As the boss, you could say well, let me look into it, or yes, it was disapproved, and I just need to do a better job of showing them why we need these changes vs. jumping in with the subordinate and railing on the higher-level boss. That just sows seeds of disregard for higher authority that won't serve you well in the long run.

What about the higher-level boss who really is a jerk? Scripture says we submit to the "masters"/bosses "who are good and considerate" as well as those "who are harsh." Man, that's a hard thing to do. I have been in those situations.

I had a boss who verbally disrespected me in front of my peers and subordinates. He openly criticized me, found fault with most things I did, and tried to take credit for anything I did well. By the grace of God, I refrained from trashing him in conversations with the people who worked for me. Instead, I had a few confidants, peers, and my wife who I could vent with to keep me sane.

There were times when that boss made changes that didn't make sense and caused hardship for my folks, and I told my guys we had to do our very best to try to support the boss and give him what he wanted. I did this while reassuring them that I would continue to try to get the boss to reconsider some of his new policies.

I'm glad I did because one of the new boss' policies that I hated the most, which was the hardest on our folks, ended up being the best thing for our unit. Our equipment downtime rates decreased significantly, and our folks maintained a consistently higher level of performance. That would have never happened if I had sabotaged the new policy by bad-mouthing the new boss' policy vs. getting behind it, supporting him, and respecting his office.

Reflection: Close your eyes and imagine the words that you have spoken about your bosses. See them flying about. Are they a swarm of circling ravens intent on

devouring your boss? Are any of the words forming prayers for your boss? Could any of them be used to prop up your boss if he/she were failing or to rally support for your boss? Consider right now how your words need to change, and imagine some of those new words coming out of your mouth.

_____
_____
_____
_____
_____
_____
_____
_____
_____
_____
_____

Philippians 2:7-8: *"But made himself of no reputation, and took upon him the form of a servant, and was made in the likeness of men: And being found in fashion as a man, he humbled himself, and became obedient unto death, even the death of the cross."*

Luke 2:49-50: *"And He said to them, "Why did you seek Me? Did you not know that I must be about My Father's business?" But they did not understand the statement which He spoke to them."*

Think of Jesus submitting to His earthly parents. I sometimes have to catch myself when dealing with people who don't get things or don't catch on as quickly as I do. I imagine Jesus and how patient he must have been with His earthly "teachers." So we also, as leaders, have to have patience and humility, realizing that some of the people that work for us don't catch on as quickly as we do.

I know that I have to realize at times that some of my abilities (mental faculties, etc.) are part of my giftings and part of the reason that I have been placed in a leadership position. There is a fine line between arrogance and recognizing your talents and abilities.

As a leader, I am supposed to use my gifts to figure out ways to serve the people who work for me (help them find their niche, reach their maximum potential, get promoted, etc.) and to guide them and the organization to success. It would be a mistake to act superior to them and lord these giftings over them.

Reflection: How is your patience looking today? Are you caustic and critical, or are you compassionate and willing to persevere with those who still haven't caught on yet? What key message, goal, etc. just doesn't seem to be getting through? What can you do to make it clearer? How can you break it down to make it more digestible? What training may be needed to help people get it at the level they need to be successful? Could it be something in the way you are communicating it? Are you using your talents to serve the people and mission of the organization, or are you looking out over them, perched on top of your talents, and lamenting over the inabilities of those around you?

_____

_____

_____

_____

_____

_____

_____

_____

_____

_____

_____

1 Corinthians 10:12: *"Therefore let him who thinks he stands take heed lest he fall."*

Industry leader. Market dominance. Award winner. No near-peer. Unrivaled. Periodically, we have to look at those areas where we are unquestionably winning and do several things.

First, we must understand <u>WHY</u> we are winning. <u>WHAT</u> exactly are we doing that is producing the success that we are enjoying? <u>WHAT</u> are we doing to make sure we keep doing what we have been doing?

Second, we must watch to see <u>WHEN</u> it is time to do something different to preserve our status as the leader. Maybe we are still the market leader or the division's top producer, but others are gaining. We must understand WHY our lead is shrinking and make the changes necessary to maintain our advantage.

Complacency is often the greatest danger we face when we get in the lead. Consider this analogy: the leader guides the team like a rudder on a ship. As the ship encounters waves and winds, a leader must find out WHERE the rudder has to be adjusted to keep the ship on course.

Reflection. Answer the applicable WHY, WHAT, and WHEN questions in this segment and reflect on WHERE the rudder may need to be carefully adjusted. Consider making this an exercise for the leadership team instead of the regularly scheduled boring staff meeting!

_____

_____

_____

_____

_____

_____

_____

25 Essential Bible Verses for Christian Business Leaders

Reflective Journal Volume 1

Chapter 3 Character

Matthew 8:5-7: *"Now when Jesus had entered Capernaum, a centurion came to Him, pleading with Him, saying, 'Lord, my servant is lying at home paralyzed, dreadfully tormented.' And Jesus said to him, "I will come and heal him."*

Any leader worth his salt shows compassion and genuine care for those under his care. This can't be taught. But if you don't have it naturally, you can pray that God would allow you to empathize with a person and give you the grace to show the necessary compassion.

Reflection: If you were to assess your personality for its capacity for compassion on a scale of 1 to 10, where would you fall, "Attila the Hun?" "Mother Teresa?"

"Ms. Indifferent?" These names were intended to bring humor, but would you want you as a boss if you were going through a crisis at home? Why or why not? Consider the actions that you have taken over the past year or two. What do those actions tell those who work for you about your capacity for compassion? Have people just stopped asking for help or stopped sharing their personal lives with you? On the flip side, are you so concerned about people's personal lives that you forget that each person must contribute a certain level of productivity if we are to be fair to all? Where and how do you strike the balance? How did you draw these lines?

_____

_____

_____

_____

_____

_____

_____

_____

_____

_____

Proverbs 4:27: *"Do not withhold good from those who deserve it when it is in your power to act. Do not say to your neighbor, come back later; I'll give it tomorrow when you now have it with you."*

Esther 6:2-3: *"And it was found written that Mordecai had told of Bigthana and Teresh, two of the king's eunuchs, the doorkeepers who had sought to lay hands on King Ahasuerus. Then the king said, 'What honor or dignity has been bestowed on Mordecai for this?' And the king's servants who attended him said, "Nothing has been done for him."*

Good Leaders are benevolent. We should be looking for opportunities to reward those who work hard for us. If we might have to stay up in the middle of the night thinking about it, so be it. That's the work of leadership.

Reflection: King Ahasuerus went out of his way to reward someone whose good work had been overlooked. Is there anyone that comes to mind that you feel may have been deserving of some reward but has been overlooked? What processes do you have in place to bring the names of deserving people in front of you? Are the processes effective in bringing the most deserving people to the forefront? Failure to do so can bring discouragement and even resentment. If secretly polled, would the people working for you feel rewarded enough? Would they consider what you labeled "rewards" as rewards to them? How big is the gap between the two, and how do you know?

_____

_____

_____

_____

_____

_____

_____

_____

_____

_____

_____

_____

_____

Proverbs 4:23: *"Above all else guard your heart for it is the wellspring of life."*

1 Sam 18:8: *"And Saul was very wroth, and the saying displeased him; and he said, They have ascribed unto David ten thousands, and to me they have ascribed but thousands: and what can he have more but the kingdom?"*

Can you handle it when your subordinates are very successful? Can you handle it when one of your subordinates is promoted to your level or even above you? If we do our job right as leaders, the people under us should grow.

We cannot be like the "wicked" "one talent" servant in the parable in Matthew 25 and leave the people we supervise in the same condition that we got them. They should be better trained and able to perform their tasks than when they started working for us. Those with the capacity for more should be groomed for more responsibility and possibly even moved on--even to the temporary detriment of our section of the company.

Steven Covey, in the book "The 7 Habits of Highly Effective People": speaks of a "scarcity mentality":

"**The Scarcity Mentality** is the zero-sum paradigm of life.

People with a Scarcity Mentality have a very difficult time sharing recognition and credit, power, or profit - even with those who help in the production. They also have a very hard time being genuinely happy for the successes of other people - even, and sometimes especially, members of their own family or close friends and associates. It's almost as if something is being taken from them when someone else receives special recognition or windfall gain or has remarkable success or achievement.

Although they may verbally express happiness for others' success, inwardly they are eating their hearts out. Their sense of worth comes from being compared, and someone else's success, to some degree, means their failure. Only so many people can be "A" students; only one person can be "number one". To "win" simply means to "beat."...It's difficult for people with a scarcity mentality to be members of a complimentary team. They look on differences as signs of insubordination and disloyalty.

The Abundance Mentality, on the other hand, flows out of a deep inner sense of personal worth and security. It is the paradigm that there is plenty out there and enough to spare for everybody. It results in sharing of prestige, of recognition, of profits, of decision making. It opens possibilities, options, alternatives and creativity.

The Abundance Mentality takes...personal joy, satisfaction and fulfillment...and turns it outward, appreciating the uniqueness, the inner direction, the proactive nature of others. It recognizes the unlimited possibilities for positive interactive growth and development, creating new Third Alternatives." (Pearson, 2011)

Reflection: Are you an insecure boss? Do you feel threatened by the abilities of your employees? What would it take for you to grow out of a "scarcity mentality" into an "abundance mentality"? How has a "scarcity mentality" affected your supervisory and other work relationships?

_____

_____

_____

_____

_____

_____

_____

_____

_____

_____

Colossians 3:23: *"And whatever you do, do it heartily, as to the Lord and not to men."*

Are you an example of the work ethic that you want your subordinates to have? Are you motivated? Enthusiastic? Or has being the "boss" become a privilege to you with special rights? Have you given yourself the "right" to come in late? To make personal calls? To become a "do as I say" vs. "do as I do" boss?

It may take the grace of God to motivate you to be enthusiastic or motivated with all the pressures you are facing, but you are there to set the example for your subordinates to follow. Nobody wants a boss that asks for more than what they are giving.

How do I get my subordinates to give their best? We all ask, "what's in for me" in some way or another. The people that work for you may say yeah, it's easy for you to be motivated you get the big bucks. Is that the only reason that you are motivated?

Reflection: Have you begun to give yourself some of the "rights" outlined above? Are you motivating your team by your example of dedication, professionalism, work ethic, and accomplishments? Have you ever thought about what's in it for your employees and checked to see if that's what they are getting? What things do you need to clean up right away regarding how you conduct yourself as the boss?

_____

_____

_____

_____

_____

_____

_____

25 Essential Bible Verses for Christian Business Leaders

Reflective Journal Volume 1

Chapter 4 Wisdom

James 1:5: *"If any of you lacks wisdom, let him ask of God, who gives to all liberally and without reproach, and it will be given to him."*

Joshua 7:3-4: *"And they returned to Joshua and said to him, 'Do not let all the people go up, but let about two or three thousand men go up and attack Ai. Do not weary all the people there, for the people of Ai are few.' So about three thousand men went up there from the people, but they fled before the men of Ai."*

James 1:5 is one of my favorite Scriptures. I remember being in a job where I was the boss of about 30 people, and I knew absolutely nothing about what they did or how to do it. It was easy in that situation to throw up my hands and say, God, I don't know what to do; please give me wisdom.

Sometimes, however, when we do have a little knowledge about something, we feel that we don't need to ask God. I guess the thought process subconsciously is that we have enough wisdom to handle it without God. THAT IS THE DUMBEST THING EVER!

God holds the entire universe in play! He is our daddy. Why would I take a test hoping to do well when I could ask my heavenly Father for all the answers? I adopted that approach long ago. I just start out in any new job by saying, God, tell me the answers about what I should do and how I should do it in this job. It has served me well. God has given me insights to pick the right goals, areas to address, where to move people, etc. Joshua was my role model for this.

Joshua was likely the greatest general in the Bible, and if you study him, all he did was ask God for the strategy for the battle and then implement it by faith. He was victorious every time. Almost.

The only time Joshua didn't have a resounding victory was when he figured he didn't need to consult God because the numbers of the enemy to be fought were so small.

It was in this "small" battle at Ai that Joshua met with defeat and even great loss of life. It's just a question of humility. Jesus, the greatest example of humility we will ever know, said I only speak what the Father has said. We don't need to have "original ideas." We can look at God's answer sheet and find the best answers every time.

Reflection: Does the idea of asking God for "the answer" sound far-fetched to you? Do you believe that you could ask God for salvation, advice on a life partner, to heal your body, and keep your children safe but not believe that you could receive wisdom from Him on small matters like which of your employees should be promoted or what your goals should be for the year? Why or why not? What is your track record in this area?

_____

_____

_____

_____

_____

_____

_____

_____

Proverbs 8:12: *"I wisdom dwell with prudence, and find out knowledge of witty inventions."*

In my definition, an invention is a new way of doing something. It may be a device, procedure, a new organizational construct, etc., anything that helps you do something better, provides better service to the customer, or streamlines how you do business.

As a young captain in the military, I began using my faith to believe God for "knowledge of witty inventions." I can testify that several times, He gave me organizational constructs that revolutionized how my work centers ran.

I remember when the senior general over information technology in our Major Command came to our base and asked me why we were organized the way we were without his permission. I had asked his office for permission but got approval from someone too junior to give it.

At any rate, he had me explain why I reorganized my flight the way I did. I briefed him on the construct. He never really gave me much feedback, but later, that general changed how all flights in the command were organized—it matched my construct.

That year, my work center won "Best Small Work Center" in the Air Force's largest Major Command, and it was in large part due to the way we were organized. When that general was promoted to a higher level, my organizational construct became how similar work centers were organized across the Air Force.

In my next job, I became chief of a Human Resource organization on a large "four-star" installation/Air Force base. I had never worked in this type of organization, but I repeated the same process of asking God for witty inventions. Again, God gave me an idea of how to reorganize the organization I was in charge of. All of my direct reports objected.

However, when I visited the other four-star Air Force bases to talk with the most seasoned of my counterparts, I found that they were all organized in the way God had shown me. My counterparts were the most seasoned leaders in the human resources career field, and their wisdom led them to reorganize in the same way God told me.

I have other examples where God gave me the idea to automate something, creatively move people around into different jobs, or revise procedures. All these inventions were received directly from my faith, believing that God could give me knowledge of "witty inventions" that would make my job easier and bring me great success.

Reflection: What area of your responsibility could benefit from a radically new way of operating? What process under your control is so convoluted, so cumbersome, such a hindrance to improved operations or customer satisfaction that it could use a "reinvention?" If you can't "believe God" for a witty invention, it is ok. How about assembling a team to tear that process apart so they can discover new ways to operate and deliver the service? Many of the improvements I have made as a leader came by assembling a team of good people and guiding/supporting them as they looked at a process or merely by being a good listener, as these good people shared their ideas on improving their work.

_____

_____

_____

_____

_____

_____

_____

_____

Proverbs 11:14: *"Where there is no counsel, the people fall, But in the multitude of counselors there is safety."*

Who is in that circle of "trusted advisors" for you? Who do you go to when you are unsure where you should start or what the best course of action is? You may think if I ask my boss too much, he may think I can't handle my job. If I ask the people who work for me, they will think I'm clueless. Along the same lines, you may think my peers are busy I won't interrupt them when I need advice. That kind of fear-based thinking will put you on an island by yourself, unable to receive the help that is readily available.

Of course, you have to know your boss and what kind of relationship you have with him. Is he trustworthy? Several times, I have had bosses who were not trustworthy. But assume for the moment that your boss already knows that you don't know everything. It's better to ask after you have done all you can on your own to figure it out than to guess or act in ignorance and then be embarrassed. Pride goes before the fall.

Similarly, the people that work for you know that you don't know everything. For many of them, it is refreshing when the boss asks for their input. It gives them a sense of value and strengthens the relationship. It doesn't mean that you will always take their suggestions and implement them as is. Their input is but one additional data point.

Another source is benchmarking, finding someone with similar processes, products, and levels of responsibility, and visiting/calling/video chatting and finding out how they do it. I have already shared that James 1:5 says, "If any of you lacks wisdom, let him ask of God, who gives to all liberally and without reproach, and it will be given to him.." You should ALWAYS ask God for wisdom. Even Solomon, the wisest man who ever lived, felt a greater safety in asking for wise counsel.

You may be thinking, why do I need wisdom from someone else if I asked God for wisdom? Well, sometimes we miss it in our hearing. It is easy to miss it when we already have a strong predisposition towards a particular course of action, i.e., when we have strong feelings one way or the other. These things cloud our ability to hear the voice of God. Wise counsel acts as a fail-safe against our natural tendencies.

Finally, if you feel the folks working for you aren't a good source of advice, train them to be. Train them on how to ask critical questions, critically evaluate options, and ask the "5 Ws" or any other method you may have that will help them bring recommendations to you that have already been thoroughly flushed out.

Reflection: What are the names of my trusted advisors? Who are some of the companies/organizations that I could benchmark with? On a scale of 1 to 10, rate your current leadership style regarding seeking the wisdom/counsel of others and God. Are you happy with that number? Why or why not? Back up your assessment with specific examples/results.

_____

_____

_____

_____

_____

_____

_____

_____

_____

_____

_____

_____

_____

_____

25 Essential Bible Verses for Christian Business Leaders Reflective Journal Volume 1

Chapter 5 Mentoring and Grooming

1 Timothy 4:12-16: *"Let no one despise your youth, but be an example to the believers in word, in conduct, in love, in spirit, in faith, in purity. Till I come, give attention to reading, to exhortation, to doctrine. Do not neglect the gift that is in you, which was given to you by prophecy with the laying on of the hands of the eldership. Meditate on these things; give yourself entirely to them, that your progress may be evident to all. Take heed to yourself and to the doctrine. Continue in them, for in doing this you will save both yourself and those who hear you."*

1 Timothy 1:18: *"This charge I commit to you, son Timothy, according to the prophecies previously made concerning you, that by them you may wage the good warfare."*

Who are you mentoring? Who are you pouring into? Who is getting the benefit of your work and life experiences? This person may not work for you. They may be in another department, perhaps even another company. As leaders, we should always be looking back to help mentor someone. Mentoring not only polishes the mentee and helps them reach their highest potential but also forces you to stay on top of your game.

Reflection: If you answered that you have no one that you are mentoring, then its time to get busy finding someone. When considering someone to mentor, there are things that you may want to prayerfully consider: growth potential, maturity, mutual interest, your availability, and what you can provide. Ask yourself if you are making mentoring decisions based on gender, attractiveness, race, age, or other factors. We are all human and, therefore, tend to act human. The trick is to keep our humanity in check by self-reflection and accountability. (For in-depth education on mentoring and grooming, please see pages 66-97 of my book "The Air Force's Black Ceiling").

_____

_____

_____

_____

_____

_____

_____

_____

_____

Genesis 41:39-41: *"Then Pharaoh said to Joseph, 'Inasmuch as God has shown you all this, there is no one as discerning and wise as you. You shall be over my house, and all my people shall be ruled according to your word; only in regard to the throne will I be greater than you.' And Pharaoh said to Joseph, 'See, I have set you over all the land of Egypt.'"*

This passage about Joseph and Pharaoh is an example of a leader giving good, talented people room to become all they can be to exercise their full potential without being threatened by their success. I can say from experience that nothing is worse than having a micromanager boss, an insecure boss, or both. Talented people need room to stretch their wings and see how far and fast they can climb.

Micromanagers are like kryptonite to these people. Allowing micromanagers to run unchallenged is the surest way to lose your most talented people. A good leader recognizes that having great people on his team makes his team successful, and everyone wins.

As the boss, I need to be secure enough to let my people flourish, knowing that I will only go as high as my team goes. Insecure, prideful, micromanaging bosses assume they have all the best answers and, therefore, have to see everything to ensure that everything is done the best way that it can be done--their way.

This management style kills the spirit and enthusiasm of those bright "Josephs" on the team. It motivates these types of people to seek opportunities somewhere else, where they can express their creativity and achieve their full potential.

Reflection: Where are the Josephs in your organization? Are you setting them over responsibilities commensurate with their ability? Do you believe that when your team does well, it's a reflection on you? Are you using your authority and resources to open doors to those who can run with their talents or enforce barriers and cumbersome "mother-may-I" approval processes? Joseph was

allowed to flourish under Potiphar and Pharoah's authority, and everything Joseph did for them prospered. Where can you reposition and unleash a "Joseph" in your organization, under your authority, to tackle a huge obstacle and score a victory for your team? Do you realize that Joseph wasn't the slave with the most longevity in Potiphar's house? Nor was he one of the seasoned leaders in Pharoah's administration. Are you afraid to unleash a Joseph, someone with unusual talent and ability, merely because of the reaction of those who have been around longer? How do you justify giving more leash to an exceptional talent while keeping a tighter rein on someone who has paid their dues and been loyal but just doesn't have the rare, unique giftings of your Joseph?

_____

_____

_____

_____

_____

_____

_____

_____
_____
_____
_____
_____
_____
_____

Luke 9:46-7: " *Then there arose a reasoning among them, which of them should be greatest. And Jesus, perceiving the thought of their heart...*"

    How do you create an environment where you encourage everyone to be their best, reward behavior, and delegate responsibility based on ability and performance, yet minimize internal strife and jealousy? First, you must be able to sense when the healthy competition has become detrimental and quickly address it.

    First, check yourself. Have I been fair? Do I show partiality? Favoritism? How do I protect against the natural human tendency to give more praise to the people that I like the most? What processes do I have in place to ensure I am aware of how well everyone on the team is doing?

No boss can know everything that each of their subordinates is doing, but what do I have in place to funnel up the good things that they are doing, the things that align with our goals?

Reflection: Where is the thermometer in your organization? How are you assessing the climate to assess how healthy it is as it relates to competition, perceptions of favoritism, and unfairness? Do you have favorites? Let me ask again: do you have favorites? Is it obvious? What checks and balances do you have in place to ensure that rewards match performance and workplace contributions, not your internal list of favorites?

_____

_____

_____

_____

_____

25 Essential Bible Verses for Christian Business Leaders Reflective Journal Volume 1

Chapter 6 Divisiveness and Proper for Authority

Numbers 12:1-15: *"Then Miriam and Aaron spoke against Moses because of the Ethiopian woman whom he had married; for he had married an Ethiopian woman. So they said, 'Has the LORD indeed spoken only through Moses? Has He not spoken through us also?' And the Lord heard it. (Now the man Moses was very humble, more than all men who were on the face of the earth.) Suddenly the LORD said to Moses, Aaron, and Miriam, 'Come out, you three, to the tabernacle of meeting!' So the three came out. Then the Lord came down in the pillar of cloud and stood in the door of the tabernacle, and called Aaron and Miriam. And they both went forward. Then He said, 'Hear now My words: If there is a prophet among you, I, the LORD, make Myself known to him in a vision; I speak to him in a dream. Not so with My servant*

Moses; He is faithful in all My house. I speak with him face to face, even plainly, and not in dark sayings; and he sees the form of the LORD. Why then were you not afraid to speak against My servant Moses?' So the anger of the LORD was aroused against them, and He departed. And when the cloud departed from above the tabernacle, suddenly Miriam became leprous, as white as snow. Then Aaron turned toward Miriam, and there she was, a leper. So Aaron said to Moses, 'Oh, my lord! Please do not lay this sin on us, in which we have done foolishly and in which we have sinned. Please do not let her be as one dead, whose flesh is half consumed when he comes out of his mother's womb!' So Moses cried out to the LORD, saying, 'Please heal her, O God, I pray!' Then the Lord said to Moses, 'If her father had but spit in her face, would she not be shamed seven days? Let her be shut out of the camp seven days, and afterward she may be received again.' So Miriam was shut out of the camp seven days, and the people did not journey till Miriam was brought in again."

The preeminent point in these Bible verses is that as a leader, you have to protect the leaders you have appointed and not let them be overrun, easily circumnavigated, or mistreated. There are several subtle sub-points in this passage that support this theme, so I want to go through them one at a time.

Miriam and Aaron spake against Moses. This passage starts with the fact that Miriam and Aaron, key leaders amongst the children of Israel, gave voice to their thoughts and feelings about Moses. Many of us have armchair quarterbacked our leaders, second-guessed their decisions, appointments, style, approach to problem-solving, etc. It's something that I have struggled with and had to keep in check. Putting your feelings and opinions out there in the atmosphere is another thing altogether.

This airing of opinions is a common problem when you have a lot of leaders and strong personalities in an organization. These leaders bring their experiences and their opinions to the workplace. The problem comes when they voice opinions contrary to those of higher-level leadership.

Has he not spoken through us also? As a leader, it's natural to analyze a situation and consider how you would approach it. It's also natural as an aspiring leader to compare yourself to the leaders above you. It goes something like this: you see a situation in the office, and you see how your boss handles it, and you say in your head "I would have handled it this way." Sounds harmless. There is, however, a very great danger in these "natural" comparisons.

One of the greatest sins ever recorded in the Bible was when the angel Lucifer compared himself to God. He forgot about the great privilege afforded him to be Heaven's praise and worship leader, and he got so caught up that he began to dream about supplanting God on His throne (Isaiah 14:4-22).

It all begins in the heart. In Isaiah 14:13-14 it says of Lucifer, "For you have said in your heart: 'I will ascend into heaven, I will exalt my throne above the stars of God; I will also sit on the mount of the congregation on the farthest sides of the north; I will ascend above the heights of the clouds, I will be like the Most High.'"

Similarly, Miriam and Aaron crossed a line where harmless musings or observations of Moses became a heart issue. In their hearts, they began to say we are on the same level in our abilities as Moses. These thoughts led to the next step: they felt they should have the same authority to speak as Moses.

Suddenly the Lord said... If you can see that divisiveness is the key issue, then you can see why the Lord spoke "suddenly" when Miriam and Aaron spoke against Moses. God had seen this scenario play out in heaven, where the divisiveness and discontent in Lucifer's heart became vocalized and later spread, resulting in division amongst the angels. The result, the Bible says in Revelations 12:4, was that Lucifer "drew a third of the angels" over to his poisoned way of thinking into rebellion against God.

As a leader in your organization, it's tough to foster the drive to improve things and encourage people at all levels to be their best and challenge the status quo while balancing the essential organizational principle of chain of command and respect for authority.

Division. It might as well be a grenade. A well-placed grenade of division will destroy a room full of unity. Unity, cohesion, and camaraderie are all essential to efficiency, productivity, and achieving the organization's vision.

It takes a strong leader to manage the dynamics of leaders leading leaders. Young leaders are like young lions. They are eager to learn how to roar, conquer things, and mark territory. Our job is to channel their leadership and give them a place and appropriate expression for it so that they don't roar at the wrong people or in the wrong settings.

I speak with him face to face. I think it's so cool how God handles this situation. In this passage, God reminds Miriam and Aaron that He picks the leaders in the organization. In Numbers 12:6-8, he says if I had picked you to be the leader, I would have told you so. God is funny. If it wasn't enough to say that He didn't pick them, he tells them why Moses is better qualified.

Paraphrasing, God says, I speak to the prophets and you in "dreams," "visions," and "dark speeches" but with Moses, I speak "mouth to mouth." Wow. That put them in their place. It's as if God said do you really want to go there? Do you want to know why Moses is more qualified than you? Here it is.

I had to take a similar approach with a strong, seasoned leader, who I thought was worth saving. He was up in arms because I selected someone other than him to fill a higher-level position in his work center. I gave this leader a detailed accounting of why the leader we were bringing in was a better fit for the job, had more relevant experience, etc. Unfortunately, that wasn't enough for him. More on that story as we go.

Why then were you not afraid to speak against My servant Moses? This quote from Numbers 12:8 is so enlightening. It speaks volumes of how seriously God takes it when someone speaks out against established authority and sows seeds of division. It's as if God was saying did you really think I was going to let you speak out against my chosen leader with no consequences?

Back to my experience with the strong leader. He started bad-mouthing the new leader that I put in place. He then launched a formal inquiry through organizational channels, stating that we mistreated him because we placed someone with less ability (in his estimation) in authority over him.

He stirred up such an uproar that I had to confront him. In effect, I asked him if he thought I would let him create such a ruckus in our organization without consequence, especially after I explained why the person we put in place was better qualified.

Would she not be shamed seven days? So, I did fire the strong leader in my example. I asked him to leave immediately. He left me no alternative because he was so adamant about being in charge even after I made it clear to him that he wasn't going to be. I had to follow through on the consequences or risk letting the division he was causing wreck our unit.

I wasn't going to say this, but he was a black guy, and the new leader was white. He was making it a race thing that we let a new white leader come in and relegated him, as a black guy, to second in command. Here's some backstory. This leader was also spreading division primarily amongst the other younger black members of our unit. He was saying that black people in the unit were being treated unfairly.

As a black leader, this was troubling for me because I felt caught in the middle. I had a responsibility to make sure the black members of my unit were not being treated unfairly, but I had a responsibility to the entire unit not to let discord go unchecked. He did raise some matters of concern, some disturbing patterns of unfairness along racial lines for minorities in our unit. I dealt with these carefully later. But in the final analysis, he stirred up a lot of racial discord, and the underlying motive, how to make himself the boss, was self-serving.

As I look back on this Scripture, I wondered was it really different than the story of Miriam and Aaron? The main reason they were upset with Moses was that he took a black wife. Their racial biases caused them to speak out against Moses as a leader.

Afterward she may be received again. My story has a happy ending. Years later, at another job assignment, that strong leader apologized to me. He said that my firing him was the best thing that could have happened to him in his career. He said It set him on a different path. It blew me away.

When I thought about that situation years ago, I was afraid to pull the trigger and fire him. Years later, I was still afraid to talk to him. I'm so grateful that I made the right decision for the benefit of the unit and for him.

**Reflection: Can you think of any examples in your organization where people are speaking out against your established leaders or sowing disunity? What action should be taken? Are there channels for people in your organization to express their concerns privately so it doesn't have to become public? Can you think of any instance where you haven't protected your direct reports from the criticism or divisiveness of people who report to them? Do you have a strong leader under you who may have offended you with their criticism, unsolicited critiques? If that leader has apologized, have you "let him back in" to your good graces? Have you decided in your mind where the line is between sowing discord and being free to express differences and frustrations? Is it your job to teach your direct reports where that line is for you?

_____

_____

_____

_____

_____

_____

_____

_____

_____

_____

1 Samuel 24:1-1: *"Now it happened, when Saul had returned from following the Philistines, that* it was told him, saying, 'Take note! David is in the Wilderness of En Gedi.' Then Saul took three thousand chosen men from all Israel, and went to seek David and his men on the Rocks of the Wild Goats. So he came to the sheepfolds by the road, where there was a cave; and Saul went in to attend to his needs. (David and his men were staying in the recesses of the cave.) Then the men of David said to him, 'This is the day of which the LORD said to you, 'Behold, I will deliver your enemy into your hand, that you may do to him as it seems good to you.' ' And David arose and secretly cut off a corner of Saul's robe. Now it happened afterward that David's heart troubled him because he had cut Saul's robe. And he said to his men, The LORD forbid that I should do this thing to my master, the LORD's anointed, to stretch out my hand against him, seeing he is the anointed of the LORD.' So David restrained his servants with these words, and did not allow them to rise against Saul. And Saul got up from the cave and went on his way. David also arose afterward, went out of the cave, and called out to Saul, saying, 'My lord the king!' And when Saul looked behind him, David stooped with his face to the earth, and bowed down. And David said to Saul: 'Why do you listen to the words of men who say, 'Indeed David seeks your harm'? Look, this day your eyes have seen that the LORD delivered you today into my hand in the cave, and someone urged urged me to kill you. But my eye spared

> you, and I said, 'I will not stretch out my hand against my lord, for he is the LORD's anointed.' Moreover, my father, see! Yes, see the corner of your robe in my hand! For in that I cut off the corner of your robe, and did not kill you, know and see that there is neither evil nor rebellion in my hand, and I have not sinned against you. Yet you hunt my life to take it.'"

This is one of my favorite passages of Scripture as it pertains to the proper heart attitude we should have toward our bosses. 1 Peter 2:18 says, "Slaves, in reverent fear of God submit yourselves to your masters, not only to those who are good and considerate, but also to those who are harsh." You couldn't get a leader who was harsher than Saul was to David. It's David's response to Saul's treatment, however that blows me away every time I read it.

David is the model for all of us to follow as we work to take our eyes off our boss and what they may be doing. David shows us that we have to believe that the Lord has our back and focus on ensuring that our heart attitude and responses are right.

The Bible says that David was "a man after God's own heart." In David's response to Saul's mistreatment, we get a glimpse into that heart. David's heart is like the heart of Jesus, "Who, when he was reviled, reviled not again; when he suffered, he threatened not; but committed *himself* to him that judgeth righteously" (1 Peter 2:23).

I'm not advising anyone to stay in a situation where a leader is abusing you (verbal abuse, sexual harassment, discrimination, asking you to do something illegal, etc.). What I am asking you to do is to keep your heart free of bitterness and other heart poisons as you navigate through the situation--whether God tells you to stay or gives you the green light to go.

I have had bosses who have tried to kill my career, discredit me, undermine me, and prevent me from receiving awards and promotions. Assignment after assignment, it seemed I kept getting the same kind of boss.

Then, one day, God showed me it was me. I was failing the test of what my heart should look like. As a result, I kept getting the same test over and over. 1 Timothy 2:1-2 says, "I exhort therefore, that, first of all, supplications, prayers, intercessions, and giving of thanks, be made for all men; for kings, and for all that are in authority; that we may lead a quiet and peaceable life in all godliness and honesty."

In Matthew 5:44, Jesus says, "But I say unto you, Love your enemies, bless them that curse you, do good to them that hate you, and pray for them which despitefully use you, and persecute you."

When I began to pray for my bosses, things started turning around. I didn't let how they were treating me determine whether I would pray for them or not. I prayed for them because God told me to in His Word. I also prayed that I would not let how they were treating me infect my heart. There is no way that I would have been able to pray for them if I had allowed what they were doing to be reflected in the condition of my heart.

Proverbs 25:21 says, "If your enemy is hungry, give him food to eat; if he is thirsty, give him water to drink. In doing this, you will heap burning coals on his head, and the LORD will reward you." It's again as if the Lord says to keep your heart pure and pray for those who mistreat you, and I will take care of them. 1 Peter 2:23 says that Jesus "committed himself to him that judgeth righteously."

While following this model of praying for my boss and letting God handle my boss, I actually saw bad ratings make it into my personnel file. I also witnessed, however, the power of those ratings get stripped as I got every job that I wanted. I received all the awards I desired, even though my bosses tried to cancel them.

I got jobs on several occasions that my immediate and often higher-level bosses directly intervened against. My heart was right before God, and He took care of the rest.

Does this sound farfetched to you? Can you imagine not trying to get even with a conniving boss? Can you imagine not bad-mouthing someone who is mistreating you? Can you imagine praying for someone who is out to get you, to harm your career? Think of the boss you have right now. Do you pray for that boss? Why or why not? Have you ever considered that God might have put you there to be a light to your boss? Can you see that your being there may serve a more significant and enduring purpose than executing the responsibilities in your job description? Take a heart inventory right now. What is in your heart toward your boss that shouldn't be? How are you going to get rid of it? Do you think David and Jesus' model for dealing with mistreatment is outdated? Do you feel better served taking matters into your own hands?

_____

_____

_____

_____

_____

_____

A Relationship With God

1. **God loves you very dearly and has an amazing purpose and plan for your life.**

*We love Him because He first loved us. **I John 4:19***

*For God so loved the world that He gave His only begotten Son, that whoever believes in Him should not perish but have everlasting life. **John 3:16***

*The thief does not come except to steal, and to kill, and to destroy. I have come that they may have life, and that they may have it more abundantly. **John 10:10***

2. **Because of sin, man is separated from God and cannot know and experience His love and purposes.**

*For all have sinned and fall short of the glory of God. **Romans 3:23***

*For the wages of sin is death, but the gift of God is eternal life in Christ Jesus our Lord. **Romans 6:23.***

3. **Jesus Christ came to earth and died on the cross for our sins. He rose from the dead and is the only way to a relationship with God. Through Jesus, we can know God's love and purpose for our life.**

But God demonstrates His own love toward us, in that while we were still sinnners, Christ died for us. **Romans 5:8**

Jesus said to him, "I am the way, the truth, and the life. No one comes to the Father except through Me. **John 14:6**

4. **Jesus invites us to open up to God and have an intimate relationship with Him.**

Behold, I stand at the door and knock. If anyone hears My voice and opens the door, I will come in to him and dine with him, and he with Me. **Revelation 3:20**

5. **Our responsibility is to believe and receive Jesus Christ as our Saviour and Lord.**

But as many as received Him, to them He gave the right to become children of God, to those who believe in His name. **John 1:12**

6. **When we receive Christ, we do so by faith, believing in what He did on the cross, not in our own ability or works.**

For by grace you have been saved through faith, and that not of yourselves; it is the gift of God, not of works, lest anyone should boast. **Ephesians 2:8-9**

7. **You can receive Christ now by faith and enter into a new relationship with God through prayer.**

If you confess with your mouth the Lord Jesus and believe in your heart that God has raised Him from the dead, you will be saved. For with the heart one believes unto righteousness, and with the mouth confession is made unto salvation. For the Scripture says, "Whosoever believes on Him will not be put to shame." For there is no distinction between Jew and Greek, for the same Lord over all is rich to all who call upon Him. For "whoever calls on the name of the Lord shall be saved." **Romans 10:9-13**

Here is a suggested prayer:

Father, I come to You in the name of Jesus Christ, and I thank You for sending Your Son to die for me. Jesus, I recognize my need for You. I thank You for dying on the cross for my sins and I open my heart to You right now. I receive your forgiveness for my sins, and I thank You for giving me eternal life. I receive you as my Saviour and Lord. I invite You to come in and be the Lord of my life. Show me Your love and lead me to become the person

You want me to be. I receive the Father's love and my adoption as Father God's child.

If this prayer echoes the desire of your heart, I invite you to pray it right now, and Jesus will come into your life as He promised.

*This segment comes from the book "God Loves Me and I Love Myself Overcoming the Resistance to Loving Yourself," written by Mark DeJesus. Copyright 2016 Mark DeJesus & Turning Hearts Ministries
www.markdejesus.com

Other Books By the Author:

Amazon
https://rebrand.ly/Ivan-Thompson-Amazon

Audible
https://rebrand.ly/Ivan-Thompson-Audible

Here is a list of the e-book & print titles that I have available on Amazon:

- *** 25 Essential Bible Verses for Christian Business Leaders**
- **25 Versículos Esenciales de la Biblia Para Líderes de Negocios Cristianos**
- ***25 Bible Verses for Dads**
- **25 Versículos Bíblicos para Papás: Un Diario de Reflexión**
- ***A Tsunami of Sadness**
- **Un Tsunami de Tristeza**
- ***Hope Deferred Overcoming Discouragement and Faltering Hope**
- **Esperanza Frustrada: Superando el Desánimo y la Falta de Esperanza**
- **Finding Next A Book of Divine Seasons**
- **Financial Testimonies Stories of God's Grace and Provision**
- **Financial Testimonies II**
- ***First Responders a Revelation of the Love of Jesus**

- Primeros en Responder: "Una Revelación del Amor de Jesús" (Spanish Edition)
- Increasing Your Skills and Abilities in Any Area
- Letters to Build a Young Man's Confidence
- *Lifesaving The Importance of Hearing the Voice of God
- PODRÍA SALVAR TU VIDA: La importancia de escuchar la voz de Dios
- *Lifesaving Volume II Hardening Your Heart to the Voice of God
- Podría Salvar Tu Vida Volumen II : Endurecer el Corazón a la Voz de Dios
- *The Bible Promises of Healing 16 Letters for Mom
- Promesas de Curación de la Biblia : 16 Cartas para Mamá
- Promesas de Curación de la Biblia Vol II
- The Making of a Great America Where the Founding Fathers and the Church Fell Short
- The Making of a Great America Uprooting the Spirit of Racism
- The Making of a Great America Made in the Image of Trump
- *You Should Detours and Distractions to Divine Destiny
- Usted Debería: Distracciones Y Desvíos Del Destino Divino
- Fit @ 50
- No Grandma It's an e-book
- The Air Force's Black Ceiling
- The Air Force's Black Pilot Training Experience

- <u>The Air Force's Black Pilot State of the Union</u>

*Also available in Spanish

Here is a list of the audiobook titles that I have available on Audible:

- The Making of a Great America: Where the Founding Fathers and the Church Fell Short
- The Making of a Great America: Made in Trump's Image
- A Tsunami of Sadness
- Financial Testimonies: Stories of God's Favor, Grace, and Provision
- 25 Essential Bible Verses for Christian Business Leaders
- 25 Versículos Esenciales de la Biblia para Líderes de Negocios Cristianos
- You Should Distractions & Detours to Divine Destiny
- Usted Debería: Distracciones Y Desvíos Del Destino Divino
- The Bible Promises of Healing 16 Letters for Mom
- First Responders a Revelation of the Love of Jesus
- 25 Essential Bible Verses for Dads
- Increasing Your Skills and Abilities in Any Area
- Letters to Build a Young Man's Confidence
- No Grandma It's an e-Book!
- The Air Force's Black Ceiling

Bibliography

DeJesus, M. (n.d.). *God Loves Me and I love Myself Overcoming the Resistance to Loving Yourself.* Columbia, SC: Mark DeJesus and Turning Hearts Ministries.

Mind Tools Editorial Team. (n.d.). *Deming's 14-Point Philosophy*. Retrieved from mindtools.com: https://www.mindtools.com/pages/article/newSTR_75.htm

Pearson, S. (2011, Jan 24). *Abundance Mentality vs. Scarcity Mentality* . Retrieved from Franklin Covey Canada : http://franklincoveystephenpearson.blogspot.com/2011/01/abundance-mentality-vs-scarcity.html

www.ingramcontent.com/pod-product-compliance
Lightning Source LLC
Chambersburg PA
CBHW021005180526
45163CB00005B/1896